"I am a human being: I regard nothing of human concern as foreign to my interests." – Terence

Paint Her in Dark Colors

Wiss Auguste

Sentinel
Creations Press

This book is a work of fiction. All names, characters, places, and incidents are either the product of the author's imagination or are used fictitiously. Any resemblance to actual persons, living or dead, events or locales is entirely coincidental.

Paint Her in Dark Colors
Copyright © 2020 by Wiss Auguste
All Rights Reserved

This book or any portion thereof may not be reproduced or used in any manner whatsoever without the express written permission of the author, except for the use of brief quotations in a book review.

Published in
New York, NY
www.wissauguste.com
Instagram @w.auguste.writes

ISBN- 978-1-7326955-4-2

To Adeline, my sweetest muse.
How dull my poems would be
If you ceased to call my dreams your home!

And to Paulette Auguste Content
Mother, O! Mother!
Although I can never repay you for the sweet gift of life,
I promise not to waste it on trivial things
And empty words.

Contents

The Tale of Mermaids – 1
Rumors – 2
Paint Her in Dark Colors - 3
Spring is Here – 4
Sacrifices - 5
Forgettable Things – 6
Mind Hunter – 7
The Evergreen – 8
Born of Storms and High Winds – 9
When a Mirror Shatters – 10
Foolish Words – 11
Chaser of Sunrises – 12
The Angel in Her – 13
Her Laughter – 14
A Fire in the Night – 15
The Wandering Shadow – 16
Of Music – 17
Fluctuating Mood – 18
Canvas – 19
Loud – 20
I Could Steal a Sun Tonight – 21
Delicate – 22
Homesick – 23
Pinkish Clouds – 24
Footsteps – 25
Of Compromises – 26
A Reminder of Mistakes Made – 27
In Hints and Semi-whispers – 28
Fallen Angels – 29
The Palms of Her Hands – 30
The Journey – 31

Pretty Things – 32
The Secrets in Our First Kiss – 33
The Sight of Her – 34
Dreamers – 35
Without Maps nor Compass – 37
Seasons – 38
If She Were a Garden – 39
The Realm of Love – 40
All Peaceful Things – 41
Hatchlings – 42
Untimely – 43
Rain Dove – 45
The Murmurs of the Sea – 46
A Minefield of Wishes Half-made – 47
She Smells like Freedom – 48
The Misty Fog – 49
The Crossing – 50
The Secrets of the Sea – 51
I Once Knew a Woman – 52
Even Butterflies Must Die – 53
The Mother of All Lies – 54
Below the Scarlet Moon – 55
Necessary Pain – 56
If Wishes Were Horses – 57
Before the Mad Weather – 58
Battle Cry – 59
Her – 60
Author's Biography - 61

The Tale of Mermaids

She undulates on the crest of the sea
like the *Wandering Albatross*,
proud
yet aware of the dangers that surround her—
And when the offshore wind blusters
she reels upon breaking waves,
so poised one would never know
of the riptide she swims against

She undulates on the crest of the sea,
despite unseen and unforeseen forces
pulling her from her shore,
pulling her
into the seabed.

The sun kisses her cheeks
before it wakes, before it sleeps.
And still,
she undulates
onto uncharted horizons

Rumors

What is tragedy

if not an ill-conceived marriage

like that of

whispers and *secrets*

lights and *shadows*

truths and *rumors?*

Paint Her in Dark Colors

Paint her in dark colors—
paint her as grim
as snowy winter nights,
a sky bereft of all pleasant hues

Sew her mistakes on her back like branding scars.
Throw her name into a whirlwind of rumors,
and watch it spin wildly.
Clothe her in ragged garbs dipped in mud,
reeking the stench of lies

Paint her in dark colors
then watch your work come undone
for she stands *Indomitable*,
wrapped in a coat of lights— *Crimson* and *Marigold*[1],
flaunting the strength written boldly on the smile she wears

---

[1] The color crimson symbolizes fire— vibrant, destructive when handled carelessly, necessary. Marigold is associated with the sun— all powerful and indispensable.

Spring is Here!

Spring is here, and you rejoice.
You praise the softness of its sun—
You fish the pond for trout and bass,
you bathe in the lukewarm streams.
You search for your easel and brushes
just to capture on your canvas
the sprouting of leaves once thought dead.
And when the Tulips begin to bloom,
no thanks to your watering skills,
you sit by, impatient,
eager to pluck stems of your choice.

But where were you in the days of Winter?
Where were you
when the sky birthed a sheet of snow
that rendered the flowerbed barren—
When the trees wept just to see tears
turn into ice alongside their trunks—
When birds trembled from the icy grip
and the not-yet butterflies froze to death in their cocoons?

Where were you when she needed you?

Sacrifices

A star-filled sky is the most beautiful thing.
It is also the saddest thing
as angels have to weep
for stars to be born

And you,
my sweetest Muse,
you carry the night's sky in your eyes—

And I wonder about
the places you have been.
I wonder about the stories and the tears
that have kept your star-filled sky so wondrous

Forgettable Things

A fifth of whiskey and a love song,
a bonfire
with embers burning red— a bitter silence
a pair of pensive eyes glaring into the flames,
smudging layers of *pretty* over sad memories

And there, an epiphany written on grey smokes—
memories are fleeting.
Memories are bound to be lost
in the emptiness of death,
bound to be carried into undeserving soils,
bound to be trapped in an urn
or dispersed as flurries of ash over some lake

An epiphany written on dying flames—
Memories are precious.
Time should not be wasted on
forgettable things:
Summertime birds that do not lull her to sleep
Sunsets too bland to soothe her racing mind
Sensual kisses that fail to awaken volcanos within her

Mind Hunters

She melted for words spoken with passion,
words from old songs
long forgotten by most men—
Old songs I sang to her offbeat,
but with much heart

She enjoyed the long nights
pleasantly spent between silk sheets
and dirty words—
soft jazz caressing the air,
the taste of whiskey leaving my lips
to hers.

but she was always the happiest
when,
fully clothed,
I explored the depth of her mind
as passionately as she did mine.

The Evergreen

I know a place,
a senescent forest benighted by hoary mists—
A wooded maze of skulls
and ash.
Apocalyptic.
Ominous.
I know a place where the scent of death
hijacks the morning breeze, and
poisonous shrubs grow wild and free
along its narrow paths.

Amidst the ruins of this apocalypse
grows a tree,
a single tree, unlike all other trees.
Tall, alone— ne'er lonesome
vibrant, grandiose, Eden-like
defiant of all seasons,
with greenery amiable to the coppery sun—
the green of *Hope*
the green that withers not.

Born of Storms and High Winds

Having been born of storms
and high winds, she was not
mere ripples
but the confusion strumming
the honey-dipped strings of her lyre
was of no fault of hers.

See, the timbre of her voice carried
the notes
of wisdom, loyalty, and trust.
Yet, as with that of storms and winds,
her melody remained unmatched—
Her serenade, misunderstood.

An orchestra of would-be kings
gathered
below her windowsill
and they all sang to her—
a discordant tune,
a cacophony of lies

When a Mirror Shatters

When a mirror shatters, its shards are the real danger—
not the noise it makes,
nor the void it leaves.
Does your reflection die when a mirror shatters?
When a pebble disrupts the surface of a lake
upon which
you had gazed for so long,
do you cease to exist?

Ah! The vagaries of *flaws*,
A blemish here, a pimple there.
A nose that is denied the attributes of beauty
by sheer caprices of one's mind.
Behold the vagaries of *flaws*!
Like a tree, or a leaf,
or a sun—
Like perfection itself

Foolish Words

There is a pestilence amongst humankind—
It is born out of desperation
and it is kept alive
by a tendency to cling onto ruinous
sentiments

There is a pestilence amongst humankind
and it thrives on not knowing;
It thrives on the doubtfulness camouflaged behind
a cloak of *maybes*—
It thrives on misused words

Some words will make you look
either foolish or brave
depending on whose ears they are whispered in—
I love you is a set of such words,
So is *I forgive you.*

Chaser of Sunrises

Dawn was the harbinger of all things soft—

Soft lights,

Soft sounds,

Soft air, untainted

And she awaited her dawn with fortitude—

With a soft tone

but strong words

and loud thoughts, unequivocally clear

Dawn was the harbinger of all things new—

Clear mind,

Clean slate,

A new path, unencumbered

The Angel in Her

I live on the edge of my fears,
but far into the night, I can hear her laugh—
Jocund, she chases fireflies
while my mind ponders on unsolvable riddles.

She kisses the demons I run from;
She dances amongst flames
I'd thought to be hellishly fiery.

The angel in her
carries happiness in her steps—
Her spirit runs wild through the night
while hopelessness plagues me

Her Laughter

Her laughter rises above all subtle sounds,
a sweet delight my ears never tire of,
a mixture of troubled past and confidence regained—
a statement of sorts,
joy reclaimed from old friends.

Her laughter rises above all subtle noise
to remind me of how lucky I am
for when she laughs,
I laugh.
And oh, she laughs often!

A Fire in the Night

"And what of her smile?" you asked.

With ample kindling,
light me a campfire on a midsummer night—
I will hear the crackling of twigs,
amplified
by the sweet poetry of the summer breeze.
I will hear the moldy logs
whistle
and resist the flames, forcing a slow burn.

Light me a campfire at January's dawn—
I'll feel its warmth on my skin
for which I will be grateful.
I will hear, in the distance,
the howling of wolves lurking for my flesh
but I will know I am safe
long as the moldy logs
whistle

What of her smile?
It is Summer's poetry—
Or a respite from the rigors of Winter.

The Wandering Shadow

A young demoiselle all alone
walked a deserted road
in the dead of night—

Her name was *Moon*.
On her path,
she met a weary shadow,
wandering alongside the road.

"What is it that you seek?"
The young demoiselle asked the shadow.
"I seek peace, ma'am. And I seek my master.
He's left me to wander these woods all alone,"
said the shadow.

"Would it make you happy if I silence
the lights
and let you find your peace in the emptiness of the night?"
asked the young demoiselle.

"But I do not exist without the lights!
In the dark, I become darkness. I become nothingness,
I become memories that die on your lips,"
said the shadow, worried.

"No,
you become free,"
whispered the young woman.

Of Music

But what is music?

Is it the melody that traps us in daydreams?

Is it an escape?

Is it the transcendence that hushes reality?

Or is it the memories that every note drags along?

The softness of a lover's touch,

or her voice,

or her glance?

To me, music is a series of recollections—

My bohemian Muse in a patchwork dungaree

and a feathered hat,

her delicate fingers thrumming

a worn-out guitar

rested on the arch of

her hip.

Fluctuating Moods

Sometimes she sits idly beneath the moonlit sky
by the slow running stream of the Harlem River
and she wonders if she will ever come across a heart
that catches the nuances of her love with ease

Yet, never has she wondered
whether she was deserving
of the love she craved.

Never has she questioned
the beauty in her fluctuating moods—
the marvel in every brushstroke
that painted her as the woman she was.

Canvas

A painting is a magical realm—
the soul of an artist,
the truths of a lover,
all mixed in coalescent paints, smeared on a canvas.

A painting knows no master—
if it pleases fate, a painting roams;
It lives in more than one heart
at once

A painting is a still image
that evolves, still—
each new set of eyes
find new meanings to it

A painting is my Muse,
free yet grounded,
private yet open,
mysterious, yet understood.

Loud

We have been conditioned to whisper our truths
in the ears of those we believe will accept them—
And that is how truths die.
Those predisposed to accept our truths
are not the ones who need to hear it

Truths ought to be boisterous,
screamed at the top of lungs
that have waited too long for their time to speak—
Lungs that no longer wait,
but take to the streets and demand to be heard.

Truths ought to no longer be whispered
but placated on the walls of abandoned buildings
and projected on windows of skyscrapers
in the heart of Manhattan

Her truths,
Their truths,
A light-spreading truth

A roaring noise that makes it impossible
for the thieves of dreams
to stay hidden
in the comforting darkness of their bigoted lies

I Could Steal a Sun Tonight

There is no warmth left in here—
Just an odd sound,
the heavy tread of a stranger's
boots
walking down the alleyway

Glints of the Moon on the wet cobblestones
invite her to venture after the stranger,
into the alleyway
but there was no warmth left there either—
Only bad memories, and crippling fears
overstaying their welcome

I could steal a sun tonight
to wrap the alleyway in bright lights
and warm, comforting words— but it would still feel cold.
As cold as this world that promised her *safety*
then failed her in every way

Delicate

There are mysteries in everything
that surrounds us—

How the wind knows to be gentle
on a moment old bird
with wings not yet grown

How lithops[2], in their brownish coat,
have learned to masquerade as blossoming pebbles
to keep dangers at bay

How the morning dew,
in its eerie promptitude,
caresses all leaves equally at every waking dawn

And how my muse's voice, so soothing,
carries effortlessly
the weight of wars fought and won

---

[2] Lithops are succulent plants that evolve to look like surrounding rocks to avoid predators

Homesick

Like a caged bird reminiscing the kindness of the draught
beneath its wide-sprawled wings,
like a sightless wanderer
condemned to only smell the beauty of Nature,
like a poet without his pen
left with only memories of a departed muse—
There was this hunger within her.

And they called it homesickness—
a longing to be elsewhere,
a memory that had claimed its place
among desires and dreams deferred.
a yearning for that place beyond the noise,
where her fears come undone
like long-tangled strings.

They called it homesickness—
that desire within,
the determination to find her way back
to her happiest self,
her most authentic self

.

Pinkish Clouds

But look! Look at these pinkish clouds!
the sky smiles at the sight of you,
the sea sings a melody channeled by waves
and mermaids dance to that tune
while the soft wind rushes through your hair

Feel the gentle waves
sneaking between your toes!
Feel the wet sand beneath your feet,
so grateful for your presence
that it saves your footprints as memories!

Ease the burden on your mind
just enough to appreciate
the song of the *Piping Plovers*—
They cheer you on just for being you;
they cheer you on just for living.

Footsteps

She wears high heels.
A sense of purpose and rebellion
lives in her footsteps

Sheer Defiance

And because of such rebellious resolve,
she has been labeled *loud—too loud*.
Yet, she never feels a need to explain
the fire in her soul
and the thunder in her steps.

Those who understand the connivance
of this world
also understand that being a rebel
is not a mere caprice of hers but a necessity—
Sheer defiance is her weapon of choice
against a world set out to deny her
of all that she is entitled to

Of Compromises

A subtle danger lurks in all the things we do,
whether it be loving or
     Caring,
building or upholding—
Such inherent fissures
in need of repair or destruction.

And amid these fissures,
we humans are a firestorm
of blithe decisions and
lessons learned.

So, on the blithe side of things,
she had tested the boundaries of leniency
to salvage a love that,
unbeknown to her,
was nibbling silently at the very fabric of her being

But on the learning side of things,
oh, on the growing side of things!
She had reclaimed every thread of
herself
through the shattering of all things beyond repair.

A Reminder of Mistakes Made

At last, the *Ghost of Yesterday*
kisses
the bruises on her right shoulder
goodbye—
For so long, she'd hauled a pretty basket
filled with promises gifted to her
by a lover.

But what are pretty words
alone
if not just petty lies?
What are thoughtful promises if left unfulfilled?
What are memories of
unrequited love
If not just reminders of mistakes made?

In Hints and Semi-whispers

I believe Nature to be secretive
and, if not the *Night Parrot*[3],
the *Arabian Babbler*[4] would agree.
It is in Nature's secrecies
that the bulk of its beauty lies.

Yet, if the ultimate fate of men
is to die,
That of secrets is to become public—
Nature often divulges its truths
in hints and semi-whispers

For instance, when one's natural habitat begins to feel
Toxic
there is a muffled voice
somewhere,
whispering
'Quickly! Evolve'

---

[3] The Night Parrot is an extremely elusive bird only sighted a handful of times a year.
[4] The Arabian Babbler is the only bird that consciously hides to copulate, very much like humans.

Fallen Angels

I have seen kingdoms crumble

from wall to wall.

I have seen the sun,

all vibrant and bright,

succumb to the movements of clouds.

The rainforest,

sometimes,

drowns in the very rain that gives it its name.

I have yet to see angels fall

from the sky.

Even with clipped wings, they soar.

The wind,

a silent ally,

carries them to safety.

The Palms of Her Hands

In the short seconds that live
between a firm grip and a soft touch,
the palm of her left hand holds a happy story—
She had grasped onto uncertain futures
and she had bruised her palms more than once.
There were scars to prove it— Faint scars,
a series of lines that came together
at the junction of her wrist.

Still, the palms of her hands
delicately
hold a happy story—
The story of busy hands, steady hands,
hands used for the crafting
of keys
to the prison of the mind.

The Journey

The driftwood dandles

to the caprices of whitewater currents—

a greyish stream,

the river that roars,

the endlessness of waterfalls.

Long,

downstream,

the driftwood travels but never sinks,

or never sinks for long.

A miniature boat of sorts,

sailing on the river that roars,

seemingly lost,

sailing towards the open sea

where freedom awaits

Pretty Things

She has been compared to moons,
constellations of stars,
stardust,
changing seasons
and field of lilies under caressing suns

What an injustice I am guilty of!
What an unforgivable sin it is
to equate my sweetest Muse
to ordinary, temporary things!

All flowers bloom just to wither
All moons, although marvelous,
only fortuitously light the sky—
And all stars, capricious fizzling sparks,
require darkness to shine

But my Muse, my sweet truth, my light—
She shines as bright in the dark
As she shines in daylight.
Her beauty blooms eternally,
like roses grown from heavenly soil

The Secrets in Our First Kiss

There is a tidal wave trapped

within my Muse—

I sense tremors in her fingertips

when she holds my hand

I sense tremors in her fingertips

when she hesitantly grabs the back of my head

in anticipation of a kiss

she equally craves and fears.

I taste tragedy on her lips— a lingering melancholy,

a vestige of the long cons played by men like me.

And her eyes, filled with forebodings,

beg me not to be like them.

The Sight of Her

Our dreams reveal our true desires,
they show us the utopia we wish we lived in—
A world where flowers grow anew
and fragrances yet unknown
tease our nostrils

But

When I awake from my slumber,
all my dreams become barely-memories.
My Muse, beside me, with our legs entangled
and our skins fused as one,
is a reality no dream can ever match

Dreamers

They sipped from the goblet of *Aphrodite*[5],

a potion only found in subterranean wells.

And they swore it had given them clarity,

a light on the path to true love—

They were mere mortals hoping for a *forever*

in every lover that crossed their path

Amongst them was my Muse,

a worshipper of love,

the resurrectionist of defunct dreams.

She infused life into my dying quill

and demanded everlasting love in return—

I was outraged by such a tall request.

"The arrogance of *forever* is a sin I shall not embrace.

Even the sky bleeds when the stars are angry—

even amongst the gods, love is fated to die,"

I said to my Muse.

---

[5] Ancient Greek goddess of love, beauty, pleasure, and passion.

"*Forever* is not a sin but an audacity

all true lovers have been guilty of,

and we speak of it with such certitude

not because we are arrogant but because we are dreamers,"

she responded, calmly.

No sweeter words

had ever been spoken to my skeptical soul;

No sound more convincing had ever graced my ears—

She offered me the love I craved in silence

but bashed actively.

"Then I shall dream with you, my love!

Let's feed our moments

with lights from bleeding skies.

Let's find our *forever* in every kiss, long or short,"

I replied to *Adeline*.

Without Maps nor Compasses

Draw me a map to her treasures—

Let me be abreast of the roads not to take,

the hurdles,

the detours,

the perils that await

And if that's not enough, just hand me a compass,

teach me north from south—

point me to her *Southern Cross*

the constellation of gods.

Point me to the *Water Bearer*, the Star of stars

But do not take offense if I willfully lose myself

on the edges of her twists and turns,

for no gadget can map

the ever-changing coordinates

to her garden of delights

Seasons

All seasons carry a sun and, on all seasons,

all noons look alike:

twinkles of light on periwinkle skies.

The only thing that changes

is the warmth on our skin—

a soft caress throughout Autumn's glee

or a scorch mark left by Summer's rage

All heartbreaks begin with a pain

that grips us at our core,

and all painful grips bring along brackish tears.

The only thing that changes

is the way we weep—

a muffled rage that chokes us in the dead of midnight

or a roaring flood of tears in which we drown ourselves

If She Were a Garden

If she were a garden,
She would have enchanted the eyes of passersby—
She would have been flowers, leaves, and sun
dancing the dance of life.

She would have been lavenders
jasmines
and daffodils.
A soft fragrance that heals all wounds the eyes cannot see.

If she were a garden, she would have been that sturdy tree
under whose shadow peace meets serenity—
She would have been then as she is now:
My garden of Eden, my haven, my heaven.

The Realm of Love

She stalks the sun in search of love—
She stalks the sun
just to pick that one moment
when every beam of light finds its place,
and every shadow vanishes
to create a magical spark in the darkness
of deluded dreams

She stalks the sun
but the love she seeks is not of this world;
magic does not live in the heart of nonbelievers

The realm of true love
hides somewhere alongside that blurred line
where the sky traces its long fingers across
the surface of the sea
and the chants of mermaids
recount stories of hearts like hers—
Stories of rebel hearts that had tasted love once
and refused to settle
for the mockery of lustful longing

All Peaceful Things

She basked in this sweet obsession for peace

and all peaceful things—

almost as if

she was overcompensating for her tumultuous past,

almost as if she wanted to make up for the joys

she had allowed fate to steal from her.

And in the absence of clatters and all distracting things,

she embraced the lonesome

wind.

Hand in hand, they danced into the night,

like snow flurries

carried by the thick mist.

Hatchlings

Ideas are many things—
They can be outgrowths of wings
on the back of a once flightless bird,
or the bulk of weights tied to the legs of a *Blue Jay*[6].
Ideas take root at the junction of our fears;
They grow into a field of lilies
or spread like ragweed.

Ideas are hatchlings
hundreds of them, thousands of them—
all of them wanting to be nurtured to maturity,
all of them aware that they will not all survive

And she combs through them all—
ridding herself of ragweed,
watering lilies to full bloom,
nurturing hatchlings into ideals

---

[6] The Blue Jay commonly symbolizes freedom, curiosity, and intelligence.

Untimely

Pearls of water slowly leak from a broken faucet

and each drip gets louder with time—

Each drop matches a tick

or a tock

as the old clock on the wall synchronizes itself

to the leaking faucet

    Drip

            Tick

   Drop

          Tock

And the dripping, and the ticking—

They teased her. They mocked her.

They tried to rush her patient thoughts

with reminders

of tasks not yet done

and plans that came undone

And the dripping, and the ticking—

They tried to rush her patient thoughts

but she listens not to their naggings.

She loses herself in the flight of foreign birds

leaping from branch to branch atop a cherry blossom tree,

unbothered by the timely movement of the sun.

Rain Dove

I once saw a rain dove

caught in a downpour,

wet wings,

wet feathers,

wet eyes,

flying against the wind

What does a rain dove do

when sadness rains from the open sky?

A rain dove sings

and flies into the downpour

until the sky runs dry

and the sun shines once more

The Murmurs of the Sea

A few seconds before the crashing of waves,
the sea murmurs sweet,
deceitful words to the shore—
as if the tide
wasn't an unfriendly guest.

As if the waves did not drag grains of sand
against their will,
far into the darkness of the sea.

As if the shoreline did not feel
the misplaced rage
of each wave

As if the shoreline
hadn't struggled to remain whole—
trusting, yet deceived at every tide
deceived by every wave,
and trusting, still.

A Minefield of Wishes Half-made

She felt it in her bones,

a pulling on the fibers of her tired muscles,

a coldness

that erodes her already weary joints,

an itch—

Not the kind of itch one just scratches away,

an itch that is flesh-deep,

a light, cursing through her veins.

An urge to achieve magical things,

to reach for magical heights

An urge to overcome her fears—

This refusal to spend

a lifetime

tiptoeing around

a minefield of wishes half-made.

She Smells like Freedom

There is a fragrance to resilience—
A soft scent
gentle, yet intoxicating
traveling on winds
like an airborne cure
to our fears

There is a fragrance to freedom—
the smell of peonies
infused with hints of glamour,
a silent poem read out loud
to all our senses.
A fragrance she exudes.

The Misty Fog

Of barely clad thighs, and hips, and breasts,

of a stranger's smile,

there are many musings yet to be written.

Is it not pleasure-filled for most men

to catch her timid glance

and hear from within

the obnoxious roar of their carnal desires?

      Yes.

Thus, I have learned to fear all thoughts

my mind birthed

between a mutual glance and a prolonged stare.

Only after the misty fog of lust

dissipated

had I ever been able to *see* her—

Beyond barely clad thighs, and hips, and breasts,

and smiles,

she was tranquility.

She was what forehead kisses are

to a troubled mind.

The Crossing

"Two tall pillars
on either side of a deceitfully peaceful lake—
Concrete walls, bricks, asphalt
laminated timber and steel ropes
hanging over a fifty-foot drop."

She harbored such a fascination for bridges,
a metaphor lost in me—
She said they were reminders of all the places traveled,
the smell of familiar flowers,
grey smokes escaping an old chimney,
a connection made and almost immediately lost

Bridges— reminders of risks taken,
leaps of faith into bottomless abysses.
a friend,
an overly friendly lover
or a lover turned foe

Reminders of places not yet traveled to,
greenery paving soils that once were fields of mud,
the warmth of safety,
the prospect of finding a happy place—
people with smiles to spare

The Secrets of the Sea

The secrets of the sea hide on the ocean's floor

and I, athirst for truths,

I free-dove into her deep blue—

The murmurs of sea maidens,

the whistling of dolphins,

the spears of sunlight piercing the dense blue,

They all led me to her abode of peace—

beneath the raging waves,

beneath the strong currents,

away from the overratedness of floating

I Once Knew a Woman

I once knew a woman who had sworn off love,
She had called it a ruse of the devil,
a hoax of the mind,
the soft rain that persists through a day of summer,
darkness disguised as light,
a melancholy drowned in falsely happy eyes—
Her name was *Healing*

I once knew a woman
who lived in the dreams of poets and painters,
she lived each day through
different brushstrokes.
Each day, she took another form
beneath the pen of a bard—
Her name was *Muse*

I once knew a woman who could harness tempest
and redraw the map of dreams.
She once turned my sadness into joy
with nothing but two words and half-a-smile.
She used magic
to decipher the riddles of life—
Her name was *Hope*

Even Butterflies Must Die

Even butterflies must die—
They know it from the day they are born.
It is the first truth they learn;
It is a freeing truth

Their lives,
a conspicuous beauty,
wrapped in subtle resilience

Their wings,
numinous patterns, circles,
oddly-shaped curves

Their flight,
soft, swift, serene
a soundless flutter into the crepuscule

Even butterflies must die—
they understand death
and once death is understood, life is understood

They always die
a beautiful death
for they always live a purposeful life

The Mother of All Lies

Fear was the mist that swathed the forest,
the fog,
the dark,
the icy grip

Fear was the nimbus clouds
that loomed;
the rain that never came

Fear was the Mother of all lies,
the slaughtering of all promising thoughts,
the mortal enemy of smiles, joy, freedom.

Fear was her enemy,
eschewed,
outcasted

Below the Scarlet Moon

There is blood in the sea,
I am certain of it—
A hint of scarlet tarnishes the white
of waves and
streams of light spills
from the wounded Moon.

And the Mother of mermaids,
she sings no more,
she waits
for her children to heal—
She sings no more, but she hums
with aching in her throat, she hums a somber tune.
She hums the hymn of helpless matriarchs
forced to watch
their children bleed from wounded egos,
forced to watch their children ache
from necessary pain.

She hums
a tune that soothes but cannot heal

Necessary Pain

Find me a tree that does not
weep
throughout a downpour!

                    Find me a leaf that's not grateful for
                              the dust
                          being washed away!

                                        Find me roots that do not
                                                rejoice
                            when raindrops end a lengthy drought!

If Wishes Were Horses

A shooting star travels

across the open sky,

for all to see and wish upon—

a trail of dust follows

And when the stardust dissipates,

people around the globe stare into the ground

and silently hope that, in the days to come,

all their wishes will come true at once

Wishes are quite a noble thing

but they will not cure the ailment of mankind—

"If wishes were horses…"[7] she whispered

as she carried the torch that will set the status quo ablaze

---

[7] "If wishes were horses, beggars would ride." – Nursery rhyme that stresses the importance of taking actions instead of simply wishing for things

Before the Mad Weather

Brisk is the wind that announces
the mad weather,
remarkable in its swiftness
as in its rage.

I read doom in the flight of birds,
a fortune written on flapping
wings
and muffled lulls

I read doom
in the words that travel
on silent roars
and foreboding gazes

Brisk is the wind that announces
the crumbling of self-proclaimed monarchs
and the rise
of once-belittled wives

Brisk is the wind
that announces the crumbling
of a status quo

Battle Cry

A bell tolling
above the mountainous suburbs
of the Americas

The sound of drums ripping
the air
from Congo to Somalia

The wailing
of conch shell horns
in the deep woods of Haiti

Battle paint smeared on cheeks
that once housed
ruined mascaras and dried up tears

And to lead them into battle, a long-haired warrior,
fiery,
atop a three-horned horse
Respect
Equality
Fairness

Her

I still have much to learn from the softness
of life
and on the subject of *Her*,
I reckon I am but a novice—
All the stories that have dripped from her
tears
carry the common themes
of *boundaries*
and *safe words*— and I have learned them all

I run amuck
through the wilderness
written in the brown of her eyes
just to catch glimpses of her,
only the glimpses
she would allow me to have— and I have kept them all

Still, on the subject of *Her*,
I remain a novice—
I dare steal modicums of intrigue from her many
mysteries
and I read all her riddles in an eternal loop,
not to seek their meanings but to bask in their beauty

Biography

Wiss Auguste was born and raised in Jacmel, a gorgeous small town located on the southernmost coast of Haiti. He began writing acrostic love poems at the age of twelve. His writing, unfortunately, hit a snag when he migrated to the United States at the age of twenty-one. He was no longer an idealistic teenager; he was a displaced young adult struggling to make life make sense. He put all self-fulfilling and creative activities on the back burner as he worked odd jobs and pursued a Bachelor's degree in Criminal Justice.

After the passing of his father, Wiss turned back to poetry to find himself and escape the burden of grief. He reconnected with his creative side, and his craft allowed him to vent freely. He hid behind his poems to show his weaknesses to the world without compromising his pride.

Wiss considers himself naturally empathetic, and his empathy fuels his writing. His poetry usually touches on mindfulness, self-expression, romantic love, self-love, growth, and the complexity of the human character. He has developed a hybrid poetic style encompassing elements from the nineteenth century's Romanticism and Symbolism. He credits the soothing musicality of his poems to his polyglot background. Unsurprisingly, his favorite poets are Paul Verlaine, Coriolan Ardouin, Arthur Rimbaud, William Wordsworth, Pablo Neruda, Emily Brontë, and Oswald Durand.

Other books by Wiss Auguste

The Illusions of Hope (Hope Series Book 1) Sentinel Creations Press, 2018
The Valley of Orchids (Hope series, Book 2) Sentinel Creations Press, 2020
Beneath the Veil of Time, (Poetry) Sentinel Creations Press, 2019

www.ingramcontent.com/pod-product-compliance
Lightning Source LLC
Chambersburg PA
CBHW022124040426
42450CB00006B/838